DORIS LESSING

DORIS LESSING

by

MICHAEL THORPE

Edited by Ian Scott-Kilvert

To Elin

PUBLISHED FOR
THE BRITISH COUNCIL
BY LONGMAN GROUP LTD

LONGMAN GROUP LTD
Longman House, Burnt Mill, Harlow, Essex

*Associated companies, branches and
representatives throughout the world*

First published 1973
© Michael Thorpe 1973

*Printed in Great Britain by
F. Mildner & Sons, London, EC1R 5EJ*

ISBN 0 582 01230 9

CONTENTS

I. LIFE AND ATTITUDES 5

II. *THE GRASS IS SINGING* AND OTHER AFRICAN
STORIES 9

III. 'CHILDREN OF VIOLENCE' 19

IV. *THE GOLDEN NOTEBOOK* 25

V. *BRIEFING FOR A DESCENT INTO HELL*;
CONCLUSION 29

A SELECT BIBLIOGRAPHY 35

DORIS LESSING

I. LIFE AND ATTITUDES

D ORIS LESSING was born of British parents in Kerman-
shah, Persia, on 22 October 1919. Her father was
then managing a bank for the Imperial Bank of
Persia; in 1924, disillusioned with business life, he made the
romantic retreat to a farm on the high veld in Rhodesia.
From Mrs Lessing's autobiographical and fictional writings
it is clear that, while the farm turned out to be no happy
haven for her parents, it became their imaginative daughter's
lucky spiritual home. A 'neurotic' child, she wasted no
more time than she could help in the classroom, at a convent
school in Salisbury. She left school at fourteen and became
a nursemaid for a time before returning to the farm. Like
Olive Schreiner, her nineteenth-century forerunner as
novelist of Southern Africa and of an isolated, aspiring
girl's life—and her fictional heroine Martha Quest—she
was formed on the one hand by her intense response to the
living body of Africa, on the other by independent reading
and reflection.

A deeply felt recollection of that early life occurs in the
second chapter of *Going Home*, an account of her last visit
to Rhodesia in 1956 (after which the Rhodesian govern-
ment did her the honour of declaring her a prohibited
immigrant). There she comments: 'The fact is, I don't live
anywhere; I never have since I left that first home on the
kopje. I suspect more people are in this predicament than
they know.' It was a house literally made of the earth to
which it had long since returned; in her loving, detailed
description of it the reader who may have begun with the
later Lessing, whose characters insecurely inhabit an urban
wilderness—'I have lived in over sixty different houses,
flats and rented rooms during the last twenty years and not
in one of them have I felt at home'—may be surprised in

working back to discover her afresh as one of the major artists of the African landscape and seasons.

Having written two bad novels on the farm and destroyed them, she returned to Salisbury in the guise of a telephone operator. Her life sharply changed direction, turning outward into the flux of the brashly provincial settlers' capital. She immersed herself, she says, in 'the kind of compulsive good time described in *Martha Quest*'. This led to marriage with a Civil Servant and the birth of a son and a daughter. This marriage broke up and she married again. Her second marriage also failed, but out of it she brought with her to England in 1949 a son and her author's name of Lessing, which was her second husband's.

Establishing herself in London was a struggle at first. In those drab post-war years it was 'a nightmare city', but so it might have seemed anyway to one who had known nothing during her first thirty years but bright light, sun and clean air. Still, it was 'the old country'; her mother was a Londoner, her father, an Essex man, had talked nostalgically of the tamed, eternally green countryside. In any case, London was the inevitable launching-point for an African writer at that time. In an autobiographical sketch opening her contribution to *Declaration* (1957), a symposium of authors' 'positions', Mrs Lessing notes that she had already written and destroyed six novels, but the one she brought with her, *The Grass is Singing*, was accepted at once and acclaimed as one of the outstanding novels by a post-war English writer. It was reprinted seven times within five months, and by 1971 the Penguin edition alone had sold 70,000 copies. Her early experiences in London were saved for semi-autobiographical treatment until *In Pursuit of the English* appeared in 1960. In tone it is the lightest of her books. By the time it appeared it could already be considered 'dated', but it remains a convincing impression of London working-class life in those grey years of post-war austerity, and well illustrates the author's insight into people's ordinary lives. The sympathetic outsider's bias is less marked than in the documentaries of George Orwell, but it is there and mention of it points to some preliminary consideration of her political and social concern.

Like Martha Quest, the heroine of her 'Children of Violence' novels, Mrs Lessing had been involved in leftist politics in Rhodesia as a Marxist but not as a card-carrying Communist. Three years after coming to England she joined the Communist Party, but although she left the Party in 1956, it was not, she has informed me, simply because of the Soviet invasion of Hungary—'I didn't leave in the sense of some dramatic event, I simply let the thing fade away . . . there were many reasons.' In 1954 her first novel dealing explicitly with Martha's political involvement, *A Proper Marriage*, had come out. Her previous books about Africa had, however, all implied a strong concern, humanitarian rather than political, to expose the sterility of white 'civilization' in Rhodesia and its unjust dealing with the African.

It must be admitted that the English reader who comes to her writing about politics with a knowledge of the literature of the thirties and forties, which reflects a similar swing from optimistic commitment to utter disillusion, will often have a sense of *déjà lu*. But it is the themes and attitudes that will seem over-familiar, not the mode of presentation. What Mrs Lessing set herself to do, she tells us in her Preface to a new edition (1972) of *The Golden Notebook*—and the statement applies equally well to the 'Children of Violence' novels—was 'to give the ideological "feel" of our mid-century'—and it is hard to think of any other English novelist who has matched her achievement in this respect. 'Dated' such work must be, as her Preface concedes, for ' "Marxism" and its various offshoots has fermented ideas everywhere, and so fast and energetically that, once "way out", it has already been absorbed, has become part of ordinary thinking'. Later in the Preface she makes the point that takes us to the heart of her political concern: 'I think it is possible that Marxism was the first attempt, for our time, outside formal religions, at a world-mind, a world ethic.' This was its appeal to her, as it was to the six famous contributors to *The God that failed*,[1] and to millions without a name.

Her search for 'a world ethic' did not end with the recognition that the Marxist 'dream' had turned into a nightmare; unlike many disenchanted writers, at no time had she compromised her artistic integrity in the service of a narrow creed. In her contribution to *Declaration*, 'The Small Personal Voice', she justly attacked critics for failing to see that the theme of 'Children of Violence' was 'a study of the individual conscience in its relations with the collective'. The Marxist word 'collective' should not mislead: the unity she seeks is older than any political dogma and is the goal of the questing artist, not the politician. She looks back in *Declaration* to the great realists, praising their 'humanity' and 'love of people'—Tolstoy, Balzac, Dostoevsky, Stendhal —and names Mann as the last of those whose work was capable of 'strengthening a vision of a good which may defeat the evil' (today she would surely add Solzhenitsyn). It may be noted that these names are all European; there is little precedent in English fiction for the kind of visionary sweep over society she aims at. Comparing the English novelists of the fifties, she criticizes their parochialism; the anti-heroes of Wain and Braine are 'petty' (her own heroine, Martha, feels alienation but fights it). She accuses the more seriously influential work of Camus, Sartre, Genet and Beckett of a 'tired pity', 'emotional anarchy' and of indulgence in 'the pleasurable luxury of despair'. Her positive claim for the novelist, on the face of it modest, in fact asks as much of him as can be hoped: 'In an age of committee art, public art, people may begin to feel again a need for the small personal voice; and this will feed confidence into writers and, with confidence because of the

[1] *The God that failed: Six studies in Communism*, by Arthur Koestler, Ignazio Silone, André Gide, Richard Wright, Louis Fischer, Stephen Spender, edited by Richard Crossman, 1950.

knowledge of being needed, the warmth and humanity and love of people which is essential for a great age of literature.'

II. *THE GRASS IS SINGING* AND OTHER AFRICAN STORIES

When it appeared in 1950 *The Grass is Singing* at once joined the company of *Heart of Darkness, Mister Johnson* and *Cry, the Beloved Country* as one of the few profound explorations of the tragedy of the white man's presence in Africa. Mrs Lessing's characteristic strength was already refined and matured. Though the subject cries out for the liberal's moral indignation, her narrative is controlled throughout. There is commentary, but we are so completely immersed in the inward study of a claustrophobic 'double solitude' ('The world was small, shut in a room of heat and haze and light') that it never obtrudes. It is restricted to the barest details and seldom does Mrs Lessing even allow herself irony; the story could speak for itself.

The epigraphs from *The Waste Land* and the 'Author Unknown' point the novel's double purpose: to show the true nature of 'white civilization' in settled Africa and to write a parable of the coming overthrow of white oppression by potential black force. To achieve these aims Mrs Lessing took the clichés of white supremacy, especially that of white infallibility, and exposed them to the implicit judgement of fallible lives. The whites can only survive so long as the fiction of infallibility sustains them, as Charlie Slatter and the Police Sergeant realize when they seek to cover up the Turners' weakness.

The Turners, neither pioneers nor Boer trekkers, represent the commonplace middle of any class or colour; lacking 'guts', they find no prop in belonging to a superior race, but above all they are cursed with fatal weaknesses of temperament. This stems from lives that have taught them a fear of insecurity and a hopeless dependence; they are temperamentally unsuited either to enter the settlers' enclave or relieve each other's loneliness. Yet they must make a pretence of strength—Mary in her fatalistic 'struggle' with her servants, Dick in imposing his will on both native and fickle land. Their shared tragedy shows them all too human: Dick lacks the absoluteness of a Charlie Slatter, who 'like the natives he despised' recklessly rapes the land, bullies his 'niggers' and passes on, seeing in Africa no abiding home. Mary and Dick, though conditioned to acceptance of their white role, are nevertheless sensitives, dreamers, whom the system cannot afford. In portraying them Mrs Lessing evokes a sympathy with which we can see them beyond the stereotype of oppressors as victims themselves—pitiably failing to live up to the inhuman image their race has created. We pity Dick, nursing his grove of young gum trees, his tribute to the land, or clutching a handful of the soil he must forsake. Mary, too, is pitiable; for her hot Africa has been the perpetual antagonist, yet the same country can offer every cool June, as it does on her last morning, a glimpse of delusory peace: 'as if she were holding that immensely pitiful thing, the farm with its inhabitants, in the hollow of her hand . . .'

The Grass is Singing, tracing every stumbling step of this couple's fated life together, builds up an almost intolerable tension like their own. We inhabit with them the heat-choked house, watch Moses, the epitome of black force, loom through Mary's eyes, feel how the bush bars escape and only waits to complete the final violation. Mary's obsession with Moses, which lesser novelists would have vulgarized, develops as in a dream; she herself never understands it. Ironically, it is with an inferior native that Mary is forced for the first time in her life—with white or black—into 'the personal relation': 'It was like a nightmare where one is powerless against horror: the touch of this black man's hand on her shoulder filled her with nausea; she had never, not once in her whole life, touched the flesh of a native.' What does Moses feel? Jealousy, clearly, of the new white assistant who stands between him and Mary, but at the end Mrs Lessing retires, like Conrad in his Malayan stories—though without Conrad's rhetoric—from the incomprehensible: 'what thoughts of regret, or pity, or perhaps even wounded human affection were compounded with the satisfaction of his completed revenge, it is impossible to say'.

The Grass is Singing was soon followed by Mrs Lessing's first collection of short stories with an African setting, This Was the Old Chief's Country (1951), Martha Quest (1952) and Five (1953)—five novelle of which four are set in Africa. (Martha Quest, the first volume of 'Children of Violence', will be discussed later.) The early African stories and novelle were in 1964 combined with other stories published or written up until 1963 to form a collection of thirty pieces entitled African Stories (for details see the Bibliography).

In a Preface to this volume Doris Lessing recalls that her first two books 'were described by reviewers as about the colour problem . . . which is not how I see, or saw, them'. The reviewers' bias was, of course, symptomatic of what was in the early fifties an awakening interest in the problem. Her deeper concern, already evident in the compassionate handling of her first novel, was with the human problem: 'colour prejudice is not our original fault, but only one aspect of the atrophy of the imagination that prevents us from seeing ourselves in every creature that breathes under the sun'. This perception is reinforced by her vision of 'Africa which gives you the knowledge that man is a small creature, among other creatures, in a large landscape'. This attitude infused her work from the beginning; only once does a narrow didacticism limit her achievement, in the long story from Five entitled 'Hunger', a failure, as she recognizes in the Preface, because she deliberately set out to write a story of social purpose. Though she is convincing in her attempt to bring us close to Jabavu's experience from primitive hut to city shebeen, the story as a whole conforms to the 'Joe comes to Jo'burg' morality tale, of the native 'child's' corruption by the evil white city. Ironically, perhaps because of its very predictability, 'Hunger' has been, she thinks, 'the most liked'.

Another reason why 'Hunger' may seem to fail is the reader's inevitable doubt about the authenticity of the white writer's adoption of the African's viewpoint. Nowhere else, if one excepts so universally intelligible a story of sexual jealousy as 'The Pig', does Mrs Lessing attempt this. As with Moses in *The Grass is Singing*, she confines herself to what she has observed and, within plausible limits, imagined. Her main business is with the white settlers she knows best; in portraying their lives she includes, but does not concentrate upon, racial problems.

In fact two thirds of the African stories are about the personal lives of the white settlers, with the natives in the background. Mrs Lessing refuses to limit herself to the doctrinaire viewpoint that because the monstrous shadow of the racial conflict blots out the African sun it is impossible to write on any other topic or to treat the white oppressor as an ordinary human being. In Africa, as elsewhere, ordinary people are preoccupied with their own loves, ambitions and dreams: great sensitivity in these areas may lie side by side with an indifference, conditioned from infancy, to the quality of the lives of those considered 'inferior'. (Consider the irrelevance of the relatively modern concept of 'social conscience' to our response to the novels of Jane Austen and much of the work of James and even George Eliot.) Few can become heroes or self-sacrificing martyrs in any condition of life—and few indeed can be masters of their own lives. The pathetic, sometimes moving, ordinariness of the supreme race is one of the abiding impressions these stories leave; in their fears and insufficiency they are simply and vulnerably human. This is brought out in a wide range of subtle studies: 'Eldorado', where the possessed dreamer represents those hundreds who fail for every one who succeeds in converting the far country into the material stuff of dreams; 'Old John's Place' and 'Getting Off the Altitude', in which the child's unblinking eye searches out the shabbiness of adult lives behind the prosperous, full-living face; 'Lucy Grange' and 'Winter in July', taut studies of the emotional cost to those numerous lonely women sacrificed to the obsessed settlers' lust for the land; and, at a lower social level, we meet in 'A Road to the Big City' the white counterparts of Jabavu, no less than he prey to a cruelly deceptive dream.

That loose political category, 'white', is broken down under the novelist's eye into a spectrum of shades of opposition and difference. Two of her most complex renderings of this awareness are 'The Second Hut' and 'The De Wets Come to Kloof Grange'. We find in these not only the traditional antagonism between Englishman and Afrikaner but a deep exploration of the pathetic inner lives of people struggling, as all do, to build themselves a secure world to live in. There are no simple contrasts. In 'The Second Hut' the English pair and the Afrikaners alike are struggling to cling to the last shreds of dignity and what they call life in an Africa—natural as well as human—bent on expelling them. Though the Van Heerdens, living 'native', obviously have the greater capacity for survival, for both pairs of white intruders the country offers only an ironic promise and fertility and a passage to a further 'grey country of poverty'. In both this story and 'The De Wets Come to Kloof Grange', as in so much of the African writing, the isolated women attract strongest feeling. Major Carruthers's wife takes to her bed, while Major Gale's has built a more soothing, but nonetheless fragile, retreat in her eighteenth-century English room and tamed two acres of garden—'she had learned to love her isolation'. Upon this intrudes the unwanted presence of the new Afrikaner overseer's young wife, Betty, bringing with her the passion and disquiet Mrs Gale has long since shed. She brings, too, a disturbing affinity for the Africa beyond the English garden,

for the river in the 'green-crowded gully', with its
'intoxicating heady smell': this Mrs Gale has learnt to ignore,
raising her gaze to '*her* hills', but to the brash girl it is
'a lovely smell' and she walks alone through the bush to
seek it rather than Mrs Gale's reluctant companionship.
Just as Van Heerden's wife in 'The Second Hut' finds
content in her drowse of children: it is they who collab-
orate, however crudely, with 'Africa', while the finer
whites pale behind their gentlemanly ideal. Mrs Gale
glimpses this truth when, after Betty has pretended to run
away, she 'hated her garden, that highly-cultivated patch
of luxuriant growth, stuck in the middle of a country that
could do this sort of thing to you so suddenly', but when
she learns the girl's flight was faked, a provoking demand
for her husband's love, she rejects her insight and labels it
'savage'. In such stories Mrs Lessing is as powerful as
D. H. Lawrence, blending revelation of her characters' inner
lives with an intense evocation of setting and atmosphere
to expose simultaneously the flaws in both character and
society.

Where Mrs Lessing does write explicitly of the 'colour
problem', what interests her most is, not the crass exercise
of white power, but the complex predicament of the 'good'
white. Excellent examples are 'Little Tembi', 'No Witchcraft for Sale' and the ironic *novella* from *Five*, 'A Home
for the Highland Cattle'. 'Little Tembi' explores the
pathetic outcome of a well-intentioned white mistress's
nursing of a sick African boy, who later develops so jealous
a dependence upon her affection that he turns into a petty
criminal, stealing to gain attention. It brings out with
moving irony the risk involved in the stock attitude the
Jane McClusters adopt when they approach the native
sympathetically—'They are just like children, and appre-
ciate what you do for them'. In 'No Witchcraft for Sale',
as in 'Little Tembi', the good mistress's humane treatment
of her cook is at bottom dangerously self-gratifying—'she
was fond of the old cook because of his love for her child'.

The cook, a 'mission boy', collaborates in his mistress's comfortable view of the white-black relation as 'God's will'. When a tree-snake spits in the little baas' eye, Gideon heals it with a mysterious root from the bush, but afterwards, when the whites want him to lead them to where it can be found, he hoodwinks them. It remains Gideon's secret, 'the black man's heritage' which lies deep below the white man's shallow possession of the land. Gideon has the last, unconsciously ironic word: 'Ah, Little Yellow Head, how you have grown! Soon you will be grown up with a farm of your own . . .'

Mrs Lessing's most sustained ironic treatment of the dilemma of the newer-minted white liberal is 'A Home for the Highland Cattle'. Marina Giles 'was that liberally-minded person produced so plentifully in England during the thirties . . . somewhere in the back of Marina's mind has been a vision of herself and Philip living in a group of amiable people, pleasantly interested in the arts, who read the *New Statesman* week by week, and hold that discreditable phenomena like the colour-bar and the black-white struggle could be solved by sufficient goodwill . . . a delightful picture'. It all comes down to something more basic—the servant problem, dear to our Victorian forebears, but which nowadays one goes abroad to encounter. While Philip, her agriculturist husband, pursues the African's well-being in his practical, worthwhile way, Marina struggles in their semi-detached box at 138 Cecil Rhodes Vista (wicked name!) to practise human equality upon her 'boy', Charlie. From the beginning Charlie is groping to comprehend this new variety of 'madam' and clearly it will not be long before he takes advantage of her weakness.

As a central serio-comic symbol Mrs Lessing has chosen one of those Victorian pictures of highland cattle ('Really, why bother to emigrate?'), left in Marina's keeping by Mrs Skinner, her landlady. Marina, naturally, abhors it, but Charlie seems to admire it—an admiration dimly connected, she supposes, with the part played by cattle in tribal life 'that could only be described as religious'. This part is the use of cattle as *lobola*, or bride-price, now as shown in this story in a pathetic state of decay. Gradually, Marina works herself into a false position: her attempts to treat Charlie more humanely 'spoil' him; she becomes so embroiled in his personal life that she lands in the ancient role of white paternalist, with the African as foolish child. Her attempt to get him married to Theresa, his pregnant girl friend, brings the picture into play. Thinking it valuable, Charlie has the bright idea of presenting it to Theresa's father in lieu of *lobola*; and Marina, betraying her white integrity, agrees to give it to him. She and Philip drive the pair and the picture out to the wretched location where the father lives, only to receive from the broken-down old man a nostalgic homily on the degeneration of the old ritual and courtesies. Nevertheless, he accepts the picture. Philip and Marina drive back, grim but little wiser, leaving the couple unbeknown to them to celebrate in an illicit liquor den. The sequel is no less sordid. When Mrs Skinner gets an inkling on her return what those 'white kaffirs' have done with her precious picture, she has no difficulty in getting Charlie arrested for stealing a few worthless objects including a 'wooden door-knocker that said *Welcome Friend*'. Later Marina, by now a truly colonial madam in a smarter suburb, passes a file of handcuffed prisoners in a street 'in this city of what used to be known as the Dark Continent', thinks she recognizes Charlie among them but, intent on discovering that 'ideal table' at once dismisses the thought. Her well-intentioned but amateurish meddling has caused both his misfortune (though he accepts it with easy philosophy) and her tired indifference. In this story, exercising a light but firm ironic control comparable to Forster's in *A Passage to India*, Mrs Lessing has, like that earlier analyst of the inner contradictions of imperialism, subtly exposed the perils of liberal efforts at 'connexion', if unsupported by extraordinary character and intelligence.

Marina is a 'liberal' outsider; if she utterly fails, what more can be expected of those who grow up conditioned to acceptance of the system? We glimpse in 'No Witchcraft for Sale' how the white child is formed to rule; he is unlikely ever to begin to imagine affinity with the native. More deeply, 'The Old Chief Mshlanga' exposes through the eyes of a sensitive, solitary girl who had herself never known any home but Africa, the ignorant assumptions that perpetuate master racism. It is an intense moment of wakening for her to realize that 'this was the Old Chief's Country' and a painful stage in her maturing to recognize her inherited guilt for dispossessing him. The child's eye view provides a naïve naturalness of response and a strong focus of values; its advantages are most fully explored in 'The Antheap', from *Five*. At its centre is a sensitive white child, Tommy Clarke, who questions the double standard he is expected to live by as he grows older; forbidden to play with 'a lot of dirty kaffirs . . . now you're a big boy', he feels something vital is lost and 'wept bitterly, for he was alone'. While his father's boss, Macintosh, grubs a fortune from the antheap, Tommy forms substitute playmates from clay and gives them names—a striking contrast in the exploitation of the African earth. One figure Tommy names Dirk—after a 'kaffir' boy whose lighter colour intrigues him. It is fitting that Dirk should be one of Macintosh's half-caste children: as the illicit bond between these boys strengthens, through their hard-won friendship Mrs Lessing is naming the price that the Macintoshes of Africa should be made to pay for their reckless abuse of the land and its people. The forced union between the two worlds has produced that most tragic being, the 'coloured', accepted by neither; he is in the flesh inextinguishable witness to the whites' double standard. In tracing the boys' love-hate relationship through the years and the baffled response of old Macintosh, Mrs Lessing concentrates on the play of emotion between groping, passionate people, letting our sense of the 'problem' emerge without insistence.

The boys' 'victory' is equivocal: 'now they had to begin again, in the long and difficult struggle to understand what they had won and how they would use it.'

'The Antheap' is the one story in which connexion is really achieved and then it is between white and coloured, not white and black—in the circumstances the only probable connexion. Elsewhere, the most that can be hoped for is a fair give-and-take in the master-servant relationship, such as exists in ' "Leopard" George' until the white master blunders ignorantly through his favourite African's sensibilities. And, ultimately, through his own: for that 'undeveloped heart' (E. M. Forster's phrase) is tragically immature, slow to grasp connexions, not non-existent. In a story similar in theme to ' "Leopard" George', but more strongly dramatized, 'The Black Madonna', Mrs Lessing uses in a way reminiscent of Forster the Italian artist Michele to point the want of 'heart' in 'a tough, sunburnt, virile, positive country contemptuous of subtleties and sensibility'. In her portrayal of the Captain we see how the double standard divides mind and heart against each other: 'You can't have a black Madonna', the Captain protests, seeing no contradiction in his assumption that you *can* have a black mistress, his 'bushwife' Nadya. 'Black peasant Madonna for black country', answers Michele simply. Under the skin the Captain senses the true meaning of this—in human as in spiritual love—but fears to let it out. So it remains at the end; Michele, like Forster's Italians, is potentially a liberating agent, but the offer is declined. The Captain, when Michele visits him in hospital, refuses to accept the picture of the black girl, but, when the white-haired Italian leaves, turns his face to the wall and silently weeps. After an acid beginning, 'The Black Madonna' develops into one of Mrs Lessing's most compassionate portrayals of the white man's tragedy. The necessity to maintain an impregnable front before 'the lesser breeds', the male drive needed to 'tame' the land, must warp the personal life at its deepest levels.

Together, *The Grass is Singing* and *African Stories* provide
a complex inner portrait of an anachronistic society, which
has failed to adjust to the pace of change; they make us see
and feel that it consists of people little different from ourselves, who demand understanding, even sympathy, as well
as judgement.

III. 'CHILDREN OF VIOLENCE'

The 'Children of Violence' quintet (1952-69) spans almost
the whole of Mrs Lessing's writing career. It takes us from
an African experience as remote and closed as that of
Schreiner's *The Story of an African Farm* through layer upon
layer of Anglo-colonial society, out of Africa altogether
to London, where her heroine's life closes in again, a life of
rooms, flats, decaying claustrophobic houses, in each phase
deepening the study of 'the individual conscience in its
relation with the collective'.

Her narrative owes nothing to structural experimentation
and supplies little debatable symbolism. As her heroine's
Bunyanesque name, Martha Quest, and the title of the
series suggest, she does not mask her intentions. Several
modern novelists, following Proust, have used the novel
sequence, centring upon one character's experience but
giving a detailed impression of movement through time.
In English we think of Ford, Waugh, Cary, Powell, Durrell,
Snow, and the form continues in Edward Upward's current
political trilogy and the work of younger novelists such as
Frederic Raphael. How can we distinguish Doris Lessing's
series from these? Most obviously, for its African subject-
matter, as a narrative of the never-to-be-repeated experience
of growing up in an isolated white settlers' enclave and
striving, like Schreiner's Lyndall in the nineteenth century,
to move outwards into a world of fuller experience and
wider values. Secondly, in centring upon a woman's
experience, to a degree unmatched since Virginia Woolf in

intensity. Further, while 'feminist' would be a less dubious label to attach to Lessing than Woolf, her fiction has *critical* relation to the question of the position of women and is no mere instrument of it. The sequence is also (like Cary's and Upward's) one of those rare works which give politics due place, without reducing the characters to puppets. All these aspects except the political (initially relatively slight) combine in the strong first volume, *Martha Quest* (1952), which covers the period from Martha's critical awakening in adolescence to her first marriage. The opening pages indicate the major themes and sketch Martha's heavy consciousness of herself—derived from books—in relation to them and the spirit of her time:

> She was adolescent, and therefore bound to be unhappy; British, and therefore uneasy and defensive; in the fourth decade of the twentieth century, and therefore inescapably beset with problems of race and class; female, and obliged to repudiate the shackled women of the past.

We watch her seeking to thrust outward away from her parents' 'ironic mutual pity' and her father's 'dream-locked' existence, but see that she is a dreamer too, and will have a hard journey toward her 'noble city' where there was 'no hatred or violence' (the traditional symbol of the ideal city lives in Martha's imagination until her death, and provides the binding symbol of the series)[1]. While lucidly defining Martha's typical dilemma Mrs Lessing nevertheless gives us a complex awareness of the 'many selves' Martha must choose from in her individual effort to take 'the responsibility of being one person, alone', together with a sympathetic insight into the baffled lives of those who surround her. Though she sees the Colony as in 'a sickness of dissolution' Martha, a child of her time and place, is infected herself. One self is drawn to the false unity, the 'system of shared emotion' of the Club—this is the modern girl who 'knew everything was allowable'; another deeper self

[1] I have discussed this at length in 'Martha's Utopian Quest', *Common Wealth*, 1972 (see Bibliography).

responds to individuals whom she sees as trying like herself to forge a painful separateness, hence the shameful affair with the despised Jew, Adolph King, and her marriage out of tenderness and a willed conviction of a shared aspiration to freedom to Douglas Knowell. Yet beneath all is a deeper self:

> . . . the gift of her solitary childhood on the veld; that knowledge of something painful and ecstatic, something central and fixed, but flowing . . . a sense of movement, of separate things interacting and finally becoming one, but greater—it was this which was her lodestone, even her conscience.

This description of Martha's 'individual conscience' is reinforced more strongly in this than in the later books by Mrs Lessing's passionate recollection of the body of Africa; it links her heroine with the Romantic impulse of aspiration toward a cosmic unity beyond the reach of any political or social idea—a link we may lose sight of as the series progresses but which the final novel confirms.

Of the first four novels, *Martha Quest* leaves the most rounded impression: we see Martha's restless development against the permanent reality of her spiritual Africa; African setting and atmosphere are dense, suggesting a true point of departure and potential return. The next three novels trace her erratic movement through flawed relationships in the makeshift colonial capital toward the desired but distant establishment of herself as a 'free spirit'—in which attempt, despite her modern advantages, she is hardly less hampered by convention and conformity than were Eliot's Dorothea or James's Isabel Archer. Disenchantment with the suburban 'bourgeois' marriage, which threatens to reduce her to wifely dependence, has become a stock theme now, but it was not so in the fifties. *A Proper Marriage* (1954) remains distinguished for its calm characterization and objective analysis of a subject too often treated with feminist indignation; we see that Douglas, no less than Martha, is the victim in this dishonest marriage, and both are guilty.

(Mrs Lessing is no bigoted feminist in her portrayals of men: compare in *The Habit of Loving* 'The Witness' and 'He', and in *A Man and Two Women* the title story and even 'One Off the Short List' with its distasteful compulsive seducer.)

At the end of the second novel Martha has shed husband and daughter and temporarily, at least, substitutes for the failed personal relationship attachment to the 'collective', influenced by the young Communists in the Royal Air Force, a new and utterly alien element in Zambesia. Though she has a brief, happy affair with one of them, *A Ripple from the Storm* (1958) mainly explores the ramifications of love for 'the people', which for Martha may also be seen as an outlet for her romantic 'passion for the absolute' (to quote the novel's epigraph from Aragon). As such, it is destined for disillusion. Unlike mid-thirties Europe, the Colony offers the tiny Communist group no footing in the 'mass'; it is cut off by ignorance and suspicion from its natural base among the Africans. Repeating recent European history, the group forms reluctant alliance with the Social Democrats and becomes fragmented, but it is the flaws within themselves that Mrs Lessing brings out so shrewdly. She shows how political purism may betray individual weakness and, in practice, destroy the individual it pretends to serve. Even Anton Hesse, who may be termed Martha's ideological second husband, a German who has suffered for his Marxist beliefs, becomes insidiously seduced by bourgeois 'furniture'. Only Athen, the doomed Greek, who is presented sympathetically but unsentimentally, possesses a felt unselfish communism. Futility is the mood of *A Ripple from the Storm* and it will repel readers who crave romance with their politics (which would have been a fictional combination indeed for that place and time); but since neo-Marxist revolutionism continues to sacrifice the individual to a 'collective' absolutism it remains a valuable cautionary tale.

While the political theme continues in *Landlocked* (1965), which covers the late forties, it is felt increasingly as mere background to Martha's revitalized emotional life. This novel is the least satisfying of the series, largely because of its very success in reflecting through a fragmented narrative the tedium and frustration, the truly 'landlocked' condition of the reactionary colonial backwater. The old political scene is dissolving and new African radicals and white extremists are taking over, but Martha has discovered love and 'from this centre she now lived'. Her love for Thomas Stern, the Polish Jewish peasant, snatched at intervals in the loft at the foot of his brother's garden, is insulated from the world of argument at first and reaches a lyrical intensity. It cannot last: Thomas, a child of violence, goes to Israel to fight for the Promised Land and when he returns is utterly changed. After his death, of blackwater fever, caught in an equivocal Kurtz-like involvement with tribal Africans, Martha has no reason to remain; her father dies too, so ending a chapter in the 'quicksand' of Martha's irritable, compassionate embroilment with her parents—which is tenderly drawn throughout the series. Martha now yearns toward the liberating sea, and beyond it England—the traditional bourne of the 'free spirit'. Africa has shrunk to a 'backdrop' of arid immensity; Zambesia is abandoned to the 'enemy', Sergeant Tressall, who is doubtless advocating a 'strong line' somewhere in Rhodesia today.

The title of *The Four-Gated City* (1969), the final volume in the series, harks back to Martha's youthful vision of a Utopian city upon the veld (suggestive in shape of Campanella's City of the Sun), but, though Africa re-appears in the prophetic Appendix as a refuge from nuclear holocaust, London is the novel's city.

At first it is shabby post-war London, physically and psychically desolate. There, inevitably, Martha seeks the working-class, the mythical 'proletariat' Africa denied; she finds them warm but depressing, no ideal beings (a realization *In Pursuit of the English* had already expressed, more lightly, in 1960). Martha's renewed quest is neither political nor sexual in emphasis: neither can 'create' her now; more active and independent than before, she embarks on inward self-exploration. Yet at the same time her life at the centre of the distraught liberal Coldridge household is a focus of widening responsibility toward and understanding of others, not an engrossment with self. There are no absolutes now, individually or collectively. The novel's great length is justified by its intensive exploration of the most complex and vital experience. Particularly impressive are the portrayals of 'this remarkable traffic between parents and children', in both Martha's last painful confrontation with her mother and the conflict between the adults and the questioning youth of the sixties, and the tracing of Martha's anguished inner probing whose pace is set for her by Mark Coldridge's 'mad' wife Lynda. Not since Virginia Woolf has an English novelist explored so thoroughly the labyrinth of the strained sensitive mind, or pleaded so strongly for a more enlightened science of the mind than a dogmatic psychiatry provides. In this area Martha's individual conscience reaches out toward a deeper connexion with the needs of the 'collective' than any abstract cause could offer, probing 'this strange disease of modern life' (Arnold's phrase) at its root. We may be unable to share Martha's new-found hope in extrasensory powers or Mrs Lessing's prophetic vision of the survival, after atomic devastation, of a scattering of 'new children' with an inborn telepathic capacity to 'see' and 'hear' more finely: 'grown up . . . mentally and emotionally . . . they are beings who include that history [of this century] in themselves and who have transcended it'. To them the dying Martha consigns the guardianship of the 'four-gated city' some future race will build. The climax offers as the only hope a faith in Evolutionism derived, in Mrs Lessing's version, not from positive Darwinism, but (as several of the novel's epigraphs indicate) from her study of Sufism[1] in the writings of

---

[1] Sufism is an Islamic form of mystical monism; in recent years it has, like Hindu mysticism, had a growing appeal in the West. See A. J. Arberry, *Sufism*, 1950.

Idries Shah. However one views this 'solution'—Shah too
closely resembles the Shaw of *Back to Methusaleh—The
Four-Gated City* is an admirable attempt to 'strengthen a
vision of a good', to make us see and feel how we do and
should live now and here. It may become Mrs Lessing's
most influential work.[1]

IV. *THE GOLDEN NOTEBOOK*

Until *The Four-Gated City* appeared *The Golden Notebook*
(1962) had stood for several years as Mrs Lessing's most
ambitious work. It may remain her best known; the
interest it has aroused as one of *the* novels of our time
accounts for its reissue in a hardback edition with a lengthy
author's preface in 1972.

In this Preface she states that her intention was to follow
the great European—not English—novelists of the last
century in producing a comprehensive work 'describing
the intellectual and moral climate' of her time, not to
produce (as weekly critics too eagerly assumed) a feminist
broadside. She had already demanded in her *Declaration*
essay, '*Why* should the sex war be offered as a serious
substitute for social struggle?' She aspired instead to meet
the need for the more varied view of the human condition
such as a Tolstoy or a Stendhal could provide. *The Golden
Notebook*, with a writer now as protagonist, is about this
need and how hard it is in our time for the novelist to meet
it. The action is a purgative process which may—or may
not—fit Anna to convey 'a vision of a good'.

Being a 'free woman' is certainly a strong twin theme—
and the more general one; it is 'the disease of women in our
time', especially for those who like Anna attempt to 'live
the kind of life women never lived before'. But this is
inseparable from the universal theme of the individual's

[1] The paragraph on *The Four-Gated City* repeats parts of my review
of the novel, 'Real and Ideal Cities', in *The Journal of Commonwealth
Literature*, July 1970.

isolation: in a world that supplies no dependable values, Anna, like Martha Quest, must make her life as she goes along, or be torn and fragmented by it. Like many people, she knows 'I'm scared of being alone in what I feel' and fears emotion in a hostile world, but as an artist, 'driven to experience as many different things as possible', she has to face the question of responsibility. If literature is concerned with the self, it is also concerned with self-control: in the beginning Anna cannot write because she fears spreading her feelings of 'disgust and futility' (contrast the contemporary anti-hero's indulged 'alienation'); by the end she has learnt to 'live through' her divided selves, 'naming' the horrors. This, for a writer, is also her duty. We do not see Anna's predicament as separate from her society, its ideals and failures; she does reflect these, the frustration and sterility of 'living like this', without 'a central philosophy', but, forced like Martha to accept the fading of the Marxist 'dream', she seeks a new centre.

Her search is reflected in the book's unusual structure, which despite its bulk is no Victorian 'baggy monster' or rag-bag of writer's scraps. There was ample precedent for dislocated narrative in such modern novelists as Gide (*Les Faux-Monnayeurs* also includes a novelist as character writing a novel about his experience within the novel), Woolf, Joyce, Huxley and, more recently, the *nouveau roman*. In *The Golden Notebook* the discontinuity reflects, not only the novelist's viewpoint, but the lack of unity in Anna's life and life as she sees it: hence her writer's 'block'. By means of the Notebooks Anna 'divided herself into four' to avoid facing up to the chaos; in one, the Blue, she tries to be honest, and this especially is in the end superseded by the Golden, 'all of me in one book'.

The Notebooks punctuate instalments of a conventional novel entitled 'Free Women', in which Anna herself is a character, using experience in the Notebooks selectively. If 'literature is analysis after the event', the Notebooks represent 'event', 'Free Women' the literature or fiction.

If we read the Notebooks, then the novel, in that order, we would see how Anna, the unblocked writer of 'Free Women', is using her fragmented experience recorded in the Notebooks, compelling it into a *positive* whole, with control, not raw subjectivity. The African material of the Black Notebook which she cannot 'use', though it describes some of her most deeply felt experience, disappears. At the centre of 'Free Women' is the Richard, Tommy, Marion triangle from which, in the Notebooks, Anna appears excessively detached. The Notebooks are used in Anna's novel as a crucial factor behind Tommy's suicide attempt—absent from the 'real', but central in the fiction: thus Tommy becomes Anna's surrogate, he goes through the experience she evaded. After his blinding, Molly comments with tragic irony, 'he's all in one piece for the first time in his life'. The suicide motif had already been approached by Ella in the Yellow Notebook 'novel', but as a fictional projection of her own despair; in placing the Notebooks as a power for evil in 'Free Women' Anna is accepting moral responsibility for them.

Previously, in the Yellow Notebook we have seen Anna trying to fictionalize her experience, making Ella a simplified, more coherent version of herself. Ella is 'not interested in politics'—all the Red material, Anna's albatross, is cast off. In this Notebook occur anticipations of themes that will be converted to positive use in the more integrated Golden Notebook: for example, Paul's image denoting his split attitude to his profession when he tells Ella, 'we are the boulder-pushers . . . we are the failures', recurs in an almost identical passage in which Anna envisions Paul and Michael merged in a single heroic figure who reassures her, 'But my dear Anna, we are *not* the failures we think we are . . .'—the boulder-pushers are needed by the prophets at the summit; finally, Anna can tell Saul that they are both 'boulder-pushers', and in doing so implicitly accepts for herself the attitude of Mathlong, the African nationalist, described in the Blue Notebook:

He was the man who performed actions, played roles, that he believed to be necessary for the good of others, even while he preserved an ironic doubt about the results of his actions . . . this particular kind of detachment was something we needed very badly at this time . . .

Anna has been blocked as a writer because excessive self-concern has distorted her vision. Parallel with this theme is her struggle toward a fulfilled love, to achieve which she must recognize, as in the artistic sphere, that she cannot 'force patterns of happiness or simple life'. In the Yellow Notebook the story Ella must write, of 'A man and a woman . . . at the end of their tether . . . cracking up because of a deliberate attempt to transcend their own limits', yet winning 'a new kind of strength', foreshadows the 'acceptance' born of Anna and Saul's stormy relationship, the subject of the unified Golden Notebook. Though the devils that dominate the first page of the Black Notebook are exorcized on the first of the Golden, this is almost the latter's solitary indication of 'happiness'. This, Anna notes, is left out, and we are caught up in the violently fluctuating emotions of two people seeking transcendence, breaking each other down, yet building out of mutual self-recognition a new acceptance and control. This is reflected in the reduction of ninety emotional pages of the Golden Notebook to barely ten in the Milt episode of 'Free Women': the Anna there, like Ella, is more 'intelligent'; Milt, like Saul, can 'name' her and she him. They part to write the works they inscribe to each other, to push their boulders as best they can; Anna (with some irony?) also to take up marriage welfare work.

If we see 'Free Women', as these comments suggest, as representing Anna's positive re-shaping of her experience, we are bound to ask how good a novel it is. Could it stand alone? It is doubtful whether this is a very useful question: we do not read it alone, but as a skeletal piece of fiction whose flesh in 'life' the Notebooks provide. They flesh in the depth and complexity of Anna's experience—most strongly evoked in many passages, especially the African

Mashopi episodes, which the selective, conventionally shaped novel omits. *The Golden Notebook* must be judged as a whole, whose aim is to explore the plight of the socially responsive and responsible writer in the phase of disorientation and alienation in which we live. The fact that it also explores in depth the dilemma of the 'free woman', woman's most intimate experience (as in the clinically faithful description of Anna's 'day', 17th September 1954), is incidental, though indispensable to this theme. Mrs Lessing's 'free spirits', no less than those of the Brontës or George Eliot, have to love and be loved: this need creates the muddle that makes them human—and humanity, no single segment abstracted from it, is the novelist's business. The fact that many readers eagerly abstracted from *The Golden Notebook* ammunition to fight their own local battles is symptomatic of the author's succeeding in what she set out to do. Her protagonist as artist is no remote being, but one who has an uncommon responsiveness to common experience; this is recorded with such fidelity that some readers have overlooked Anna Wulf's primary significance *as artist*—if this is lost sight of it is impossible to respond adequately to the novel's larger meaning.

V. *BRIEFING FOR A DESCENT INTO HELL*; CONCLUSION

The Golden Notebook could only be done once. Having made a statement which throws serious doubt on the value of art, the artist might be expected to fall silent. Nevertheless, Mrs Lessing, like her fictional 'creature', has continued boulder-pushing. We have already considered *Landlocked* and *The Four-Gated City*, the novels that followed *The Golden Notebook* in the sixties. In these we can trace an intensifying concern with exploring the mind's frontiers: relatively limited in *Landlocked*, in the episode of Thomas Stern's paranoia and breakdown before death, this becomes

central in the inner Golden Notebook, where Anna and
Saul break down into each other and form new self-
knowing personalities and in the characterization of Lynda
and of Martha's arduous struggle to achieve self-transcend-
ence in *The Four-Gated City*. Looking further back, we can
see early indications of this development in the portrayal
of the unbalanced Mary in *The Grass is Singing* and in the
fluid presentation of Martha's many selves in the earlier
novels of the series. (Outside the novels it is at the heart of
the African stories about lonely women and is strongly
sustained in such later 'English' stories as 'To Room
Nineteen'—in *A Man and Two Women*.) It is not, therefore,
surprising that this novelist so often loosely associated with
such rationalist obsessions as Marxism and Feminism chose
in 1971 to publish *Briefing for a Descent into Hell*, a
concentrated study of a middle-aged man's mental 'breakdown' and, reflecting her interest in the ego-extinguishing
inward vision of Sufism, his confrontation with the God
within.

The 'descent' motif, symbolizing man's perilous exploration of inner space in his search for truth, is, of course, as
old as literature. The novel's title points back to the heroic
journeys to the Underworld of classical literature; in
modern times, the fictional prototype is Dostoevsky's
Notes from the Underground (1864), followed by variations
in Kafka, Conrad, Beckett, Camus and many more. Today,
under the ever-increasing evidence of 'civilized' man's
tragic self-division, few themes are more compelling for
the responsible novelist than the dubious meanings of
'sanity' and 'normality'; he is strongly supported in this by
the work of humanist psychologists like Jung and, more
recently, Michel Foucault and R. D. Laing.

In *Briefing for a Descent into Hell* Mrs Lessing cast as
protagonist an outwardly successful and established Professor of Classics, Charles Watkins. We meet him confined
to an observation ward, suffering from amnesia. Under
sedation, cut off from the social world that gave him

identity, he undergoes an inner voyage of great imaginative richness, which explores the horrors of his journey, and its 'risks' of transcendental illumination. In these dreams the perfect city is threatened (as was Martha's) by Yahoo-like creatures that inherit and—like us—degrade it. From above, borne by a blessed White Bird, he looks down upon a warring Earth exposed beneath the Moon's full light, then undergoes a descent into corruption and possible forgetfulness. Interspersed with these inner searchings are the disconsolate voices of Drs X and Y, who label his dreams religious paranoia and labour to restore his sense of 'reality': their role, like Mother Sugar's in *The Golden Notebook*, is treated critically as undermining in its attempt to explain away the individual pain by means of a witchcraft of rationality. To Watkins his dreams form a vision of 'Knowing. Harmony. God's law', but he cannot cling to the fable. His doctors probe after his outer identity, recruiting through letters the witness of wife, colleagues, friends. These demonstrate both how little he had liked or communicated with others and throw ironic light upon the idea of 'personality'. The most significant letter, in Watkins' pocket when he is found, is from Rosemary Baines, a woman who had seen him only once, lecturing in a humdrum local hall, but who was moved by some submerged quality in him. It is this quality, unexplored by his outer self, that his 'schizophrenia' offers him a chance to approach —but the ego has its defences. Self-deceivingly, Watkins submits to shock treatment, hoping to 'remember properly', but as another intuitive observer, the patient Violet Stoke, fears, it turns out 'just that—you are Professor Watkins'. 'Sanity' triumphs and Watkins, 'in possession of his faculties again', writes letters in his turn, disengages himself from Rosemary Baines and returns to the insincerities of his outer life.

Briefing for a Descent into Hell is no mere casebook (it may be contrasted in this respect with the fragmentary account of Charles's real namesake, Jesse Watkins's 'ten-day voyage' in R. D. Laing's *The Politics of Experience*). The fabular night journey within is a vividly imagined divided universe in which anarchy and harmony blend, dissolve and confront each other in dynamic tension. Counterpointed against this are the studied rationalizations of the doctors and the self-entangled prejudices of the 'normal'. If, compared to previous novels, it seems under-dramatized, this serves the purpose of deepening her protagonist's isolation. It is a novel strong and forceful in both theme and structure, as economical and self-contained as *The Grass is Singing*.[1]

Recalling her first novel in relating it to her latest points the consistency of Mrs Lessing's twin concern with the individual in himself and in relation to society, achieving in her best work insight simultaneously into the private life and the 'wider public life' by which, George Eliot commented in *Felix Holt*, the private is 'determined'. *The Golden Notebook* is the modern counterpart to *Middlemarch*. Like Eliot, Doris Lessing does not shrink from earnestness and unblushing didacticism, and though (especially in her 'English' short stories) she more often lightens her narrative with a teasing humour she frequently employs a similarly authoritative, astringent irony. Like Eliot, too, she insists on keeping absolute values before us. So serious and prolific a writer, always responsive to the pressure of the time, is likely to be uneven. In this brief introduction I have chosen to emphasize the best, omitting consideration of certain works I regard as by-products of her main effort: these include the contrived and novelettish *Retreat to Innocence* and the plays which, though lively enough, present too neatly attitudes that are rendered with more convincing complexity in the fiction (contrast, for example, the similar characters and plot in *Each His Own Wilderness* and *The Golden Notebook*). Nor have I stressed the lapses, even in her best work, into protracted documentary or circumstantial

---

[1] This discussion of *Briefing for a Descent into Hell* repeats parts of my two reviews of the novel in *Encounter*, September 1971, and *The Journal of Commonwealth Literature*, June 1972.

narrative and slack, unrevised prose. Ultimately, these
defects matter little, because of the power of the mind that
creates. Mrs Lessing is worthy to be spoken of in the
company of those great novelists before her who used the
novel, not to divert with a sensational or æsthetic experience, but to change us—Eliot, Hardy, Conrad,
Lawrence. If she shares with them also—as with her nearest
comparable contemporary, Patrick White—the unevenness
of writers who reach for the utmost inclusiveness, this is
redeemed by the unteachable quality of keeping the reader
morally alive. No English novelist today is more responsibly
concerned with keeping literature in touch with life, as it
is and as it should be.

If the reader fears that in her last two novels Mrs Lessing's
growing sense of the transcendent 'absolute' may lead her
to shed common reality, he may be reassured by her latest
collection of stories, *The Story of a Non-Marrying Man*
(1972). In the longest of these, 'The Temptation of Jack
Orkney', she creates a protagonist for whom, as for Charles
Watkins (and the author herself, in some readers' eyes), 'to
get God, after a lifetime of enlightened rationalism, would
be the most shameful of capitulations'. At the time of his
father's death, Jack begins to feel death's meaning truly and
to find his inner emptiness choked with horrors; the message
is not insisted upon, we are simply taken to the point where
Jack's temptations may (like St Antony's?) nourish new
life—or may not. The solid realities of death and misunder-
standing in the family are never lost sight of. Outside this
further strong exploration of her 'new' area of concern,
Mrs Lessing ranges across many themes and subjects: 'An
Old Woman and Her Cat' is a deeply felt but unsentimental
sketch of a homeless old woman's dogged evasion of society's
efforts to put her and her pet 'to sleep'; 'Not a Very Nice
Story' is a mordant dissection of the lies and deceptions of
four 'kind people' in love ('We feel, therefore we are'); in
'Report on the Threatened City' she channels a shrewd
analysis of the insanity of our insouciant acceptance of

inevitable annihilation through the progress reports of invisible visitors from another planet.

The Story of a Non-Marrying Man proves that her versatility of manner and viewpoint show no signs of contraction, though it must be admitted that in this collection, as in earlier ones, there are pieces that seem makeweight.

DORIS LESSING

A Select Bibliography

(Place of publication London, unless stated otherwise)

Bibliography:

DORIS LESSING: A bibliography, compiled by C. Ipp; Johannesburg (1967).

'A Doris Lessing Checklist', ed. S. R. Burkom, *Critique*, XI, i, 1968
—includes guidance to reviews.

Collected and Selected Works:

AFRICAN STORIES (1964)
—contains the short stories in *This Was The Old Chief's Country* reprinted, together with the African stories from *The Habit of Loving* and *A Man and Two Women* and the four *novelle* fro m *Five* with an African setting ('The Other Woman' omitted); also included are 'Traitors', first printed in *Argosy*, May 1954, 'The Black Madonna', from *Winter's Tales*, 1957, and two early stories, 'The Trinket Box' and 'The Pig', printed for the first time.

MARTHA QUEST and A PROPER MARRIAGE (1965).

CHILDREN OF VIOLENCE (1966-)

NINE AFRICAN STORIES, selected by M. Morland (1968)
—from *African Stories*, with an introduction by the author written in 1967.

Separate Works:

THE GRASS IS SINGING (1950). *Fiction*

THIS WAS THE OLD CHIEF'S COUNTRY (1951). *Short Stories*

MARTHA QUEST (1952). *Fiction*
—'Children of Violence', Vol. I.

FIVE: Short novels (1953)
—'A Home for the Highland Cattle', 'The Other Woman', 'Eldorado', 'The Antheap', 'Hunger'.

A PROPER MARRIAGE (1954). *Fiction*
—'Children of Violence', Vol. II.

RETREAT TO INNOCENCE (1956). *Fiction*

'Myself as Sportsman', *New Yorker*, XXXI, 21 January 1956. *Personal narrative*

THE HABIT OF LOVING (1957). *Short stories*
GOING HOME (1957). *Personal narrative*
—revised ed., 1968.
'The Small Personal Voice', in DECLARATION, ed. T. Maschler (1957)
—gives her writer's 'position'.
A RIPPLE FROM THE STORM (1958). *Fiction*
—'Children of Violence', Vol. III.
EACH HIS OWN WILDERNESS (1959). *Play*
—published in *New English Dramatists*, three plays introduced and
edited by E. M. Browne.
FOURTEEN POEMS; Northwood (1959).
IN PURSUIT OF THE ENGLISH: A Documentary (1960). *Personal narrative*
THE GOLDEN NOTEBOOK (1962). *Fiction*
—new ed., with author's Preface, 1972.
PLAY WITH A TIGER: A Play in three acts (1962).
'Footnote to *The Golden Notebook*', interview by R. Rubens, *The
Queen*, 21 August 1962.
A MAN AND TWO WOMEN (1963). *Short stories*
'What Really Matters', *Twentieth Century*, 172, Autumn 1963.
[Interview by R. Newquist], *Counterpoint* (New York), 1964.
LANDLOCKED (1965). *Fiction*
—'Children of Violence', Vol. IV.
PARTICULARLY CATS (1967). *Personal narrative*
'Talk with Doris Lessing', interview by F. Howe, *The Nation*, 204,
6 March 1967.
'Afterword', in THE STORY OF AN AFRICAN FARM, by O. Schreiner;
Connecticut (1968).
THE FOUR-GATED CITY (1969). *Fiction*
—'Children of Violence', Vol. V.
BRIEFING FOR A DESCENT INTO HELL (1971). *Fiction*
'Scenarios of Hell', interview by L. Langley, *Guardian Weekly*, 24
April 1971.
'In the World, Not of it', *Encounter*, Vol. XXXIX, ii, August 1972
—an article on Sufism.
THE STORY OF A NON-MARRYING MAN (1972). *Short Stories*.

Some Biographical and Critical Studies:

POSTWAR BRITISH FICTION: New Accents and Attitudes, by J. Gindin
(1962)
—contains a chapter 'Doris Lessing's Intense Commitment'.

CONTEMPORARY BRITISH NOVELISTS, ed. C. Shapiro; Carbondale, Illinois (1965)
—includes 'Doris Lessing: the Free Woman's Commitment', by P. Schlueter.
DORIS LESSING, by D. Brewster; New York (1965).
AFRICA IN MODERN LITERATURE, by M. Tucker; New York (1967).
' "Only Connect": Form and Content in the Works of Doris Lessing', by S. R. Burkom, *Critique*, XI, 1, 1968.
COMMON WEALTH, ed. Anna Rutherford; Aarhus (1972)
—contains 'Martha's Utopian Quest (Doris Lessing's 'Children of Violence' Quintet)', by M. Thorpe.

WRITERS AND THEIR WORK

General Surveys:
THE DETECTIVE STORY IN BRITAIN:
Julian Symons
THE ENGLISH BIBLE: Donald Coggan
ENGLISH VERSE EPIGRAM:
G. Rostrevor Hamilton
ENGLISH HYMNS: A. Pollard
ENGLISH MARITIME WRITING:
Hakluyt to Cook: Oliver Warner
THE ENGLISH SHORT STORY I: & II:
T. O. Beachcroft
THE ENGLISH SONNET: P. Cruttwell
ENGLISH SERMONS: Arthur Pollard
ENGLISH TRANSLATORS and
TRANSLATIONS: J. M. Cohen
ENGLISH TRAVELLERS IN THE
NEAR EAST: Robin Fedden
THREE WOMEN DIARISTS: M. Willy

Sixteenth Century and Earlier:
FRANCIS BACON: J. Max Patrick
BEAUMONT & FLETCHER: Ian Fletcher
CHAUCER: Nevill Coghill
GOWER & LYDGATE: Derek Pearsall
RICHARD HOOKER: A. Pollard
THOMAS KYD: Philip Edwards
LANGLAND: Nevill Coghill
LYLY & PEELE: G. K. Hunter
MALORY: M. C. Bradbrook
MARLOWE: Philip Henderson
SIR THOMAS MORE: E. E. Reynolds
RALEGH: Agnes Latham
SIDNEY: Kenneth Muir
SKELTON: Peter Green
SPENSER: Rosemary Freeman
THREE 14TH-CENTURY ENGLISH
MYSTICS: Phyllis Hodgson
TWO SCOTS CHAUCERIANS:
H. Harvey Wood
WYATT: Sergio Baldi

Seventeenth Century:
SIR THOMAS BROWNE: Peter Green
BUNYAN: Henri Talon
CAVALIER POETS: Robin Skelton
CONGREVE: Bonamy Dobrée
DONNE: F. Kermode
DRYDEN: Bonamy Dobrée
ENGLISH DIARISTS:
Evelyn and Pepys: M. Willy
FARQUHAR: A. J. Farmer
JOHN FORD: Clifford Leech
GEORGE HERBERT: T. S. Eliot
HERRICK: John Press
HOBBES: T. E. Jessop
BEN JONSON: J. B. Bamborough
LOCKE: Maurice Cranston
ANDREW MARVELL: John Press
MILTON: E. M. W. Tillyard

RESTORATION COURT POETS:
V. de S. Pinto
SHAKESPEARE: C. J. Sisson
CHRONICLES: Clifford Leech
EARLY COMEDIES: Derek Traversi
LATER COMEDIES: G. K. Hunter
FINAL PLAYS: F. Kermode
HISTORIES: L. C. Knights
POEMS: F. T. Prince
PROBLEM PLAYS: Peter Ure
ROMAN PLAYS: T. J. B. Spencer
GREAT TRAGEDIES: Kenneth Muir
THREE METAPHYSICAL POETS:
Margaret Willy
WEBSTER: Ian Scott-Kilvert
WYCHERLEY: P. F. Vernon

Eighteenth Century:
BERKELEY: T. E. Jessop
BLAKE: Kathleen Raine
BOSWELL: P. A. W. Collins
BURKE: T. E. Utley
BURNS: David Daiches
WM. COLLINS: Oswald Doughty
COWPER: N. Nicholson
CRABBE: R. L. Brett
DEFOE: J. R. Sutherland
FIELDING: John Butt
GAY: Oliver Warner
GIBBON: C. V. Wedgwood
GOLDSMITH: A. Norman Jeffares
GRAY: R. W. Ketton-Cremer
HUME: Montgomery Belgion
SAMUEL JOHNSON: S. C. Roberts
POPE: Ian Jack
RICHARDSON: R. F. Brissenden
SHERIDAN: W. A. Darlington
CHRISTOPHER SMART: G. Grigson
SMOLLETT: Laurence Brander
STEELE, ADDISON: A. R. Humphreys
STERNE: D. W. Jefferson
SWIFT: J. Middleton Murry
SIR JOHN VANBRUGH: Bernard Harris
HORACE WALPOLE: Hugh Honour

Nineteenth Century:
MATTHEW ARNOLD: Kenneth Allott
JANE AUSTEN: S. Townsend Warner
BAGEHOT: N. St John-Stevas
BRONTË SISTERS: Phyllis Bentley
BROWNING: John Bryson
E. B. BROWNING: Alethea Hayter
SAMUEL BUTLER: G. D. H. Cole
BYRON: I, II & III: Bernard Blackstone
CARLYLE: David Gascoyne
LEWIS CARROLL: Derek Hudson
COLERIDGE: Kathleen Raine
CREEVEY & GREVILLE: J. Richardson
DE QUINCEY: Hugh Sykes Davies

DICKENS: K. J. Fielding
EARLY NOVELS: T. Blount
LATER NOVELS: B. Hardy
DISRAELI: Paul Bloomfield
GEORGE ELIOT: Lettice Cooper
FERRIER & GALT: W. M. Parker
FITZGERALD: Joanna Richardson
ELIZABETH GASKELL: Miriam Allott
GISSING: A. C. Ward
THOMAS HARDY: R. A. Scott-James
          and C. Day Lewis
HAZLITT: J. B. Priestley
HOOD: Laurence Brander
G. M. HOPKINS: Geoffrey Grigson
T. H. HUXLEY: William Irvine
KEATS: Edmund Blunden
LAMB: Edmund Blunden
LANDOR: G. Rostrevor Hamilton
EDWARD LEAR: Joanna Richardson
MACAULAY: G. R. Potter
MEREDITH: Phyllis Bartlett
JOHN STUART MILL: M. Cranston
WILLIAM MORRIS: P. Henderson
NEWMAN: J. M. Cameron
PATER: Ian Fletcher
PEACOCK: J. I. M. Stewart
ROSSETTI: Oswald Doughty
CHRISTINA ROSSETTI: G. Battiscombe
RUSKIN: Peter Quennell
SIR WALTER SCOTT: Ian Jack
SHELLEY: G. M. Matthews
SOUTHEY: Geoffrey Carnall
LESLIE STEPHEN: Phyllis Grosskurth
R. L. STEVENSON: G. B. Stern
SWINBURNE: H. J. C. Grierson
TENNYSON: B. C. Southam
THACKERAY: Laurence Brander
FRANCIS THOMPSON: P. Butter
TROLLOPE: Hugh Sykes Davies
OSCAR WILDE: James Laver
WORDSWORTH: Helen Darbishire

Twentieth Century:
CHINUA ACHEBE: A. Ravenscroft
W. H. AUDEN: Richard Hoggart
HILAIRE BELLOC: Renée Haynes
ARNOLD BENNETT: F. Swinnerton
EDMUND BLUNDEN: Alec M. Hardie
ROBERT BRIDGES: J. Sparrow
ANTHONY BURGESS: Carol M. Dix
ROY CAMPBELL: David Wright
JOYCE CARY: Walter Allen
G. K. CHESTERTON: C. Hollis
WINSTON CHURCHILL: John Connell
R. G. COLLINGWOOD: E. W. F. Tomlin
I. COMPTON-BURNETT:
          R. Glynn Grylls
JOSEPH CONRAD: Oliver Warner
WALTER DE LA MARE: K. Hopkins

NORMAN DOUGLAS: Ian Greenlees
LAWRENCE DURRELL: G. S. Fraser
T. S. ELIOT: M. C. Bradbrook
T. S. ELIOT: The Making of
  'The Waste Land': M. C. Bradbrook
FIRBANK & BETJEMAN: J. Brooke
FORD MADOX FORD: Kenneth Young
E. M. FORSTER: Rex Warner
CHRISTOPHER FRY: Derek Stanford
JOHN GALSWORTHY: R. H. Mottram
WM. GOLDING: Clive Pemberton
ROBERT GRAVES: M. Seymour-Smith
GRAHAM GREENE: Francis Wyndham
L. P. HARTLEY: Paul Bloomfield
A. E. HOUSMAN: Ian Scott-Kilvert
TED HUGHES: Keith Sagar
ALDOUS HUXLEY: Jocelyn Brooke
HENRY JAMES: Michael Swan
PAMELA HANSFORD JOHNSON:
          Isabel Quigly
JAMES JOYCE: J. I. M. Stewart
RUDYARD KIPLING: Bonamy Dobrée
D. H. LAWRENCE: Kenneth Young
C. DAY LEWIS: Clifford Dyment
WYNDHAM LEWIS: E. W. F. Tomlin
COMPTON MACKENZIE: K. Young
LOUIS MACNEICE: John Press
KATHERINE MANSFIELD: Ian Gordon
JOHN MASEFIELD: L. A. G. Strong
SOMERSET MAUGHAM: J. Brophy
GEORGE MOORE: A. Norman Jeffares
J. MIDDLETON MURRY: Philip Mairet
R. K. NARAYAN: William Walsh
SEAN O'CASEY: W. A. Armstrong
GEORGE ORWELL: Tom Hopkinson
JOHN OSBORNE: Simon Trussler
HAROLD PINTER: John Russell Taylor
POETS OF 1939-45 WAR: R. N. Currey
ANTHONY POWELL: Bernard Bergonzi
POWYS BROTHERS: R. C. Churchill
J. B. PRIESTLEY: Ivor Brown
HERBERT READ: Francis Berry
FOUR REALIST NOVELISTS: V. Brome
BERNARD SHAW: A. C. Ward
EDITH SITWELL: John Lehmann
KENNETH SLESSOR: C. Semmler
C. P. SNOW: William Cooper
MURIEL SPARK: Patricia Stubbs
SYNGE & LADY GREGORY: E. Coxhead
DYLAN THOMAS: G. S. Fraser
G. M. TREVELYAN: J. H. Plumb
WAR POETS: 1914-18: E. Blunden
EVELYN WAUGH: Christopher Hollis
H. G. WELLS: Montgomery Belgion
ARNOLD WESKER: Glenda Leeming
PATRICK WHITE: R. F. Brissenden
ANGUS WILSON: K. W. Gransden
VIRGINIA WOOLF: B. Blackstone
W. B. YEATS: G. S. Fraser